To the women and girls traveling miles, climbing mountains and kicking up dust — J.F.F.

Dedicated to the women illustrators and creatives paving the way — A.K.

ACKNOWLEDGMENTS

A very special thank you to the Van Buren family, especially Rhonda and Bob, who so graciously shared time, stories and their family's treasured legacy.

Published in Canada and the U.S. by Kids Can Press Ltd.
25 Dockside Drive, Toronto, ON M5A 0B5

Kids Can Press is a Corus Entertainment Inc. company

www.kidscanpress.com

The artwork in this book was drawn in ink and colored digitally in Photoshop.
The text is set in Supernett.

Edited by Patricia Ocampo
Designed by Andrew Dupuis

Printed and bound in Dongguan, Guangdong, P.R. China, in 10/2022 by Toppan Leefung

CM 23 0 9 8 7 6 5 4 3 2 1

LIBRARY AND ARCHIVES CANADA CATALOGUING IN PUBLICATION

Title: The Van Buren Sisters vs. the pants police / written by J.F. Fox ; illustrated by Anna Kwan.
Other titles: Van Buren Sisters versus the pants police
Names: Fox, Jennifer, 1976– author. | Kwan, Anna, 1991– illustrator.
Series: Head-to-head history.
Description: Series statement: Head-to-head history | Includes bibliographical references.
Identifiers: Canadiana 20220246408 | ISBN 9781525302480 (hardcover)
Subjects: LCSH: Van Buren Sisters — Political activity — Juvenile literature. | LCSH: Women motorcyclists — Political activity — United States — History — 20th century — Juvenile literature. | LCSH: Women motorcyclists — United States — History —20th century —Biography — Juvenile literature. | LCSH: Motorcyclists — Political activity — United States — History — 20th century — Juvenile literature. | LCSH: Motorcyclists — United States — History — 20th century — Biography — Juvenile literature. | LCSH: World War, 1914–1918 — Women — United States — Biography — Juvenile literature. | LCSH: Women's rights — United States — History — 20th century — Juvenile literature. | LCSH: Clothing and dress — Social aspects — United States — History — 20th century — Juvenile literature. | LCGFT: Biographies.

Classification: LCC GV1060.2.A1 F69 2023 | DDC j796.7/50922 — dc23

Kids Can Press gratefully acknowledges that the land on which our office is located is the traditional territory of many nations, including the Mississaugas of the Credit, the Anishnabeg, the Chippewa, the Haudenosaunee and the Wendat peoples, and is now home to many diverse First Nations, Inuit and Métis peoples.

We thank the Government of Ontario, through Ontario Creates; the Ontario Arts Council; the Canada Council for the Arts; and the Government of Canada for supporting our publishing activity.

HEAD-TO-HEAD HISTORY

THE VAN BUREN SISTERS

VS.

THE PANTS POLICE

J. F. Fox

Anna Kwan

Kids Can Press

Meet Adeline and Augusta Van Buren.

Born in New York in the late 1800s, the sisters were related to the eighth president of the United States, Martin Van Buren.

And to dress head to toe in all manner of cumbersome clothing.

Adeline and Augusta Van Buren had *very different* ideas.

Before we zoom off on a truly epic adventure with these spirited sisters, let's throw it in reverse.

Addie and Gussie's mother died when they were quite young. Their father, Frank, raised the girls and their brother, Albert, to be confident, competitive and capable, and to share his love of sports.

Addie and Gussie were skilled at many sports —

skating ...

swimming and diving ...

even boxing.

By 1913, a new century had come roaring in, and for Addie and Gussie a new favorite sport reigned supreme — MOTORBIKING!

MOST UNLADYLIKE!

Zooming around town, the sisters had little
time for stuffy opinions or frilly fashions.

In 1914, war broke out in Europe. Addie, Gussie and the rest of the world watched and waited. If the United States joined in the fight, the sisters believed women should join, too.

You see, women were not allowed to fight as soldiers, but the Van Burens thought women would make excellent battlefield messengers.

To prove their point, Addie and Gussie decided to bike from New York to California — a daunting journey of about 6500 kilometers (4000 miles).

They chose the Fourth of July, 1916, to begin their ride.

It would be a hard trip. The sisters had to pack carefully. Addie, a skilled mechanic, selected tools for emergency repairs. The sisters also chose special clothing.

GOGGLES
FOR DUST
AND SANDSTORMS

LEATHER
COATS
FOR
WIND, RAIN
AND FLYING GRAVEL

LEATHER
PANTS
FOR EASY
MOVEMENT
AND POSSIBLE FALLS

HOLD UP THERE, LITTLE LADY, DID YOU SAY ... PANTS?!

You didn't think they'd ride cross-country in big swishy dresses, did you?

When the day came, Addie and Gussie were revved up and ready to show America what they could do. Decked out in their smart leather riding gear, they zoomed off from Sheepshead Bay, Brooklyn.

COAST TO COAST

In New York City people had seen everything, but when the trouser-wearing sisters rolled into towns across the country, they kicked up dust and a whole lot of fuss!

All eyes were on Addie and Gussie as they greeted locals, spoke to reporters and posed for pictures.

But not *everyone* was excited about what the Van Buren sisters were doing — or what they were wearing.

But a small-minded sheriff didn't stand a chance with these two savvy sisters.

Their father had taught them well both in the boxing ring and out. Addie and Gussie could give as good as they took, whether a boxing match *or* — in this case — a battle of wits.

The Van Buren sisters were stopped for wearing "men's" clothing again ...

and again ...

and again ...

and again ...
and again ...
and again.

But did Addie and Gussie let that stop them?

WHAT DO YOU THINK?

On September 2, 1916, two months after they'd begun their journey, the Van Buren sisters rode into San Francisco, California.

WOMAN CAN IF SHE WILL!

These sisters certainly *HAD* — riding well over 8000 kilometers (5000 miles) and proving that women were indeed *more* than capable on motorbikes.

And they hadn't let any frilly fashions — or stuffy opinions — stop them.

If the Van Burens' ride wasn't inspiration enough, Addie went on to become a lawyer.

And Gussie? She became a pilot and joined the Ninety-Nines, a women's flying club whose members included Amelia Earhart.

Yes ma'am, the sky was the limit for the Van Buren sisters.

As for the pants police?

They

became

a much

smaller

problem.

THE VAN BUREN SISTERS vs. HISTORY

Adeline and Augusta's ride was both historic and harrowing, lasting two months and covering over 8000 kilometers (5000 miles). Along with conflicts about their clothing, the sisters battled storms, rut-filled unpaved roads and mud as thick as molasses. Some days they were so dog-tired they fell asleep while riding and fell off their bikes. The Van Burens rode on, challenging 19th-century beliefs that a lady should stay corseted, covered up and at home. How did the Van Buren Way challenge the Old Way? And how far have women come today? See what you think.

THE OLD WAY

- *Quiet* — Women were *not* to be loud, express their opinions or act boldly.
- *Domestic* — Common roles for women were mostly in the home (such as wife, mother, nanny, cook, maid).
- *Private* — Ladies were not to go out in public often or to attract attention.

THE VAN BUREN WAY

- *Assertive* — The sisters were confident and bold whether in the boxing ring or on the open road.
- *Adventurous* — Riding cross-country or flying a plane, the Van Burens were daredevils.
- *Public* — Addie and Gussie didn't shy from the attention of the press or townsfolk.

PAVING THE WAY

- Though setbacks put Addie and Gussie behind schedule, when they saw the majesty of the Rocky Mountains in Colorado, they set their minds to summiting Pikes Peak, riding 4300+ meters (14 000+ feet) to the top, a new first for women on motorbikes.

- In 2002, the American Motorcyclist Association inducted Addie and Gussie into their Hall of Fame, and in 2016 — on the 100th anniversary of their trip — family, friends and admirers held a memorial ride retracing their route. Many of the riders were women.

STUCK IN A RUT

- Though not always enforced, laws against dressing as "the opposite sex" and women wearing pants persisted. While some women began wearing them more openly in the 1930s and '40s, it wasn't until around the 1960s that pants became more widely accepted as women's wear.

- Despite the Van Buren sisters' heroic efforts to show how women could serve in war efforts as motorcycle messengers, women were not officially allowed to join the U.S. military until many years later, in 1948. Today, top-ranking positions in the military are still largely dominated by men, and in many other professions women continue to struggle for equal promotions and pay.

GLOSSARY

Amelia Earhart: a pioneer in women's aviation and the first female to fly an airplane solo across the Atlantic Ocean (in 1932)

assertive: bold, forceful or confident

britches: pants; from the old word "breeches"

cumbersome: bulky, awkward or hard to manage

daunting: scary, hard or challenging

domestic: having to do with home life, or work in the home

feminine: traits traditionally thought of as female or ladylike

garments: clothing

masculine: traits traditionally associated with males

revved (up): increased in speed or energy

savvy: clever or wise

small-minded: not open to other ideas or opinions

SOURCES

PRINT

Fleming, Charles. "Sisters Ride Again: 100 Years Later, Another Group of Women Motorcyclists Go Cross Country." *Los Angeles Times*, July 30, 2016.

"Girl Motorcyclists Climb Pike's Peak." *Boston Post*, August 27, 1916.

Kekis, John. "Honoring Two Sisters' Cross-Country 1916 Motorcycle Trek." *The Paducah Sun*, July 17, 2016.

Miller, Steve. "Biking Duo Blazed Trails for Women." *Rapid City Journal*, August 2, 2003.

Murphy, William M. *Grace and Grit: Motorcycle Dispatches from Early Twentieth Century Women Adventurers*. Michigan: Arbutus Press, 2012.

"Plan Motorcycle Tour: Two Sisters to Cross Continent on Indian Motorcycles." *The Baltimore Sun*, July 16, 1916.

Ruderman, Anne Tully. "The Daring Escapade of 1916." *Ms.* (magazine), February 1978.

Smith, Catherine, and Cynthia Greig. *Women in Pants: Manly Maidens, Cowgirls, and Other Renegades*. New York: Abrams, 2003.

"To Cycle Continent: Van Buren Sisters Will Motor from Sheepshead to Golden Horn." *Brooklyn Times Union*, July 3, 1916.

"Two Girls, Attired as Men, Travel on Motorcycles." *Chicago Tribune*, July 16, 1916.

Van Buren, Adeline. "How Van Buren Girls Started for Coast." *Motorcycle Illustrated*, July 20, 1916.

"Women at Last Have Won the Right to Wear Pants: But It Still Creates Talk ..." *The Brooklyn Daily Eagle*, January 8, 1938.

DIGITAL

"Arresting Dress: A Timeline of Anti-Cross-Dressing Laws in the United States." *PBS News Hour Weekend*, May 31, 2015. https://www.pbs.org/newshour/nation/arresting-dress-timeline-anti-cross-dressing-laws-u-s.

Giordano, Ashley. "Pioneers of Moto History: The Van Buren Sisters' 1916 Ride Across America." Expedition Portal, July 4, 2021. https://expeditionportal.com/pioneers-of-moto-history-the-van-buren-sisters-1916-ride-across-america/.

Housman, Justin. "The Van Buren Sisters Were Tough-As-Nails Suffragist Moto Pioneers." *Adventure Journal*, July 4, 2019. https://www.adventure-journal.com/2019/07/the-van-buren-sisters-were-tough-as-nails-suffragist-moto-pioneers/.

Semon, Craig S. "Motorcyling Trailblazers." *Telegram & Gazette*, August 27, 2016 (updated August 28, 2016). https://www.telegram.com/story/news/2016/08/28/northboro-man-pays-tribute-to-motorcycling-sisters-from-century-ago/25561594007/.

Van Buren, Robert. "90th Anniversary Ride." 2016. https://www.vanburensisters.com/90th-anniversary-ride.

NOTES

1. Among sources, some discrepancies exist in the sisters' exact departure date for their ride. Some sources cite July 4, 1916 (the date originally planned by the Van Burens), while others claim bad weather forced them to push back to July 5.

2. Though sources say Adeline and Augusta were arrested for wearing pants, no official police records exist. The sisters were not formally arrested, but rather stopped and given warnings by police, as noted in oral accounts from Adeline recorded by her daughter Anne Tully Ruderman.